MARK BARTLETT

Can We Trust Jesus?

A Family Advent Adventure!

Can We Trust Jesus?
A Family Advent Adventure!

ISBN: 978-1-09839-420-2

Contents

Can We Trust Jesus?
A Family Advent Adventure

In many ways, the Bible is a BIG story—it starts at a place where everything WAS perfect, with people whom God created and loved, and it ends at a place where everything WILL BE perfect, with people whom God will love forever. In between these two perfect places is an amazing story.

Part of this story is about how we, people whom God loves, struggle to trust Him. And the struggle is considerable, because we believe that we can make our life work better than God can, and we make decisions thinking our way is better. People have clung to this type of choice from the time of Garden of Eden, where everything started off perfect. It is these bad choices that have resulted in a world that is broken and needs fixing. These choices have also resulted in our lives being broken, so broken that we can't fix them on our own. We need to be rescued from all the problems that have developed in and around us.

The main message of the Bible is how God fixes all that we have broken, including ourselves, to get us back to the perfect place that He had created in the beginning. At the very heart of this amazing story of the Bible is Jesus. But to connect with God and be fixed, we need to answer a very important question, "Can we trust Jesus?" If we need fixing, we need to be able to trust the one who says He can fix us.

This Advent Adventure is a "five-legged journey" that anyone can use to listen to a man named Matthew as he tries to help people see that the story of Jesus is the story of the whole Bible. Learning from Matthew is important because he, like us, was broken and needed fixing. He had seen Jesus in person, and he wrote down all his experiences to help us see the evidence Jesus provided for all his claims. Matthew reminded us of the predictions that God gave through the prophets of the past. He also told us that those predictions and promises actually came true in the life of Jesus. Hence, we can see with a lot of evidence that Jesus is trustworthy, and that he can fulfill the promises made for times ahead.

Here is the map for our adventure:

Leg One—He Arrives! (Days 1–4)

Leg Two—He Has a Message (Days 5–9)

Leg Three—He Is Different than Expected (Days 10–14)

Leg Four—He Is Rejected (Days 15–19)

Leg Five—He Is Not Done (Days 20–24)

How you might use this study guide

The "Leg" structure of the study guide is intended to follow different phases of Jesus' life. The basic premise for each day remains that Jesus fulfilled what God had foretold. As Jesus' life progresses, the events range from a miraculous birth to crucifixion and finally to resurrection. At the end of each "Leg," there is a summary that focuses on that phase of Jesus' life. You may want to use this summary to "put the pieces together" in a way that explains the story in a better way.

Each day of each Leg has a similar format. The basic structure in sequence is: what was prophesied or promised, how Jesus fulfilled that, and then some questions or discussions to talk through why that topic is important. Depending on the age group of those who will be working with this study guide, you can consider a number of ways to engage the whole family in a daily discussion. Some ideas might be:

- Take turns reading the passages.

- Designate a "teacher" who gets to ask the questions for each day.

- Appoint a person each day as the "reporter" who must summarize what happened that day for the audience.

- Provide papers and crayons to younger children and have them draw a picture of that day's events.

- Some days have a tool for parents where activities can be used to help the words and message get expressed through a learning exercise.

Most of all, have fun!

First Leg–He Arrives!

DAY ONE

What did God promise?

Again the Lord spoke to Ahaz: "Ask a sign of the Lord your God; let it be deep as Sheol (or Hades) or high as heaven. But Ahaz said, "I will not ask, and I will not put the Lord to the test. And he (Isaiah) said, "Hear then, O house of David! Is it too little for you to weary men, that you weary my God also? Therefore the Lord himself will give you a sign. Behold, the virgin shall conceive and bear a son, and shall call his name Immanuel."

Isaiah 7:10–14

The kingdom of Judah was the southern part of Israel. Ahaz, the king of Judah, was in serious danger. The northern kingdom of Israel had entered a military partnership with Assyria, and the combined armies were forcing Judah to submit to their reign. Assyria was an extremely powerful and dangerous enemy.

While Ahaz was being threatened, God spoke to him through Isaiah (the prophet) and said, "Ask me for anything, and I will give it to you, so you can trust the fact that I will protect you from your enemies." And to make Ahaz understand that God was able to deliver, He told Ahaz to ask for something as big as he could imagine.

Ahaz responded, "Don't worry, God, I am not going to put you to the test." Although Ahaz's response may seem like he was being nice and was trusting God, he was really saying that he didn't want to ask God for anything because he had already stopped trusting God. He didn't want to risk a test of God because he had already made up his mind about what he wanted to do—to enter a partnership with Assyria.

Since Ahaz wanted to do it his way and had decided to not put God to the test, God put one on himself by declaring that the sign of his power will be the birth of a child through a virgin, and that baby will be called "Immanuel," which means "God is with us."

What did Matthew tell us?

Now the birth of Jesus Christ took place in this way. When his mother Mary had been betrothed to Joseph, before they came together she was found to be with child from the Holy Spirit. And her husband Joseph, being a just man and unwilling to put her to shame, resolved to divorce her quietly. But as he considered these things, behold, and angel of the Lord appeared to him in a dream, saying, "Joseph, son of David, do not fear to take Mary as your wife, for that which is conceived in her is from the Holy Spirit. She will bear a son, and you shall call his name Jesus, for he will save his people from their sins. All this took place to fulfill what the Lord had spoken by the prophet:

Behold, the virgin shall conceive and bear a son, and they shall call his name Immanuel (which means, God with us).

When Joseph woke from sleep, he did as the angel of the Lord commanded him: he took his wife, but knew her not until she had given birth to a son. And he called his name Jesus.

Matthew 1:18–25

This is one of the most important truths in the Bible. Jesus was this unique combination of both God and man. He needed to be both so that he would truly represent us as people who need to be rescued AND at the same time be God, so he was qualified to deal with the sin that had infected humans.

Some things to discuss

Ahaz struggled to trust God. He didn't think that God could help him defeat all the enemies who were surrounding him. Why can it be so hard to trust God?

What was the uniqueness and importance of Jesus' birth?

When is it hardest for you to trust someone?

DAY TWO

What did God promise?

Now muster your troops, O daughter of troops; siege is laid against us; with a rod they strike the judge of Israel on the cheek. But you, O Bethlehem Ephrathah, who are too little to be among the clans of Judah, from you shall come forth for me one who is to be ruler in Israel, whose coming forth is from of old, from ancient days. Therefore he shall give them up until the time when she who is in labor has given birth; then the rest of his brothers shall return to the people of Israel. And he shall stand and shepherd his flock in the strength of the LORD, in the majesty of the name of the LORD his God. And they shall dwell secure, for now he shall be great to the ends of the earth. And he shall be their peace.

Micah 5:1–5a

Micah was also a prophet who lived around the same time as that of Isaiah. His message focused on the theme of justice. Judah was experiencing good economic times, but the Assyrian threat was rapidly growing. Micah wanted the people to see that the risk of Assyria conquering Israel was not related to Assyria's strength but instead was related to their lack of faith in the Lord. The sins of the nation deserved judgment and God could bring in anyone, even the Assyrians, to carry out the just consequences for the people's sins.

But Micah doesn't stop with just that warning. He goes on to talk about a "Shepherd-King," who would rise, restore, and lead the nation. In the passage above, Micah is introducing this "Shepherd-King," and is telling the people that though he would belong to the line of David (from old, ancient days), he would come from a very small, rural town, about 20 miles from Jerusalem. This promise was held on to very tightly by the Jewish leaders because it not only stated the location of this king's birth but also promised that he, as a king, would restore the kingdom as they had under David. This passage was of great importance for people of Jesus' time.

What did Matthew tell us?

Now after Jesus was born in Bethlehem of Judea in the days of Herod the king, behold, wise men from the east came to Jerusalem, saying, "Where is he who has been born king of the Jews? For we saw his star when it rose and have come to worship him." When Herod the king heard this, he was troubled, and all Jerusalem with him; and assembling all the chief priests and scribes of the people, he inquired of them where the Christ was to be born. They told him, "In Bethlehem of Judea, for so it is written by the prophet: 'And you, O Bethlehem, in the land of Judah, are by no means least among the rulers of Judah; for from you shall come a ruler who will shepherd my people Israel.' "

Matthew 2:1–6

Notice how detailed Matthew is in helping us understand that Jesus is the one whom God had promised long ago. He reminds us that where Jesus was to be born wasn't too small a detail to help us see how specific God was in telling his people about what to look for in the One he would send.

Some things to discuss

You can imagine how much "hope" Micah's prophecy would have given to the people of Israel. However, it had been over 700 years since he had given those people that promise! What do you think people of Jesus' time would be thinking when they heard about this newborn in Bethlehem?

Putting the ideas of a "shepherd" and a "king" together seems unusual. A king is very powerful, and a shepherd is considered as having a very humble job. Try and explain how those two contrasting things could be true of one person.

Ideas for parents: Make a morning promise to your children that you will give them a treat at the end of the day. See if they remember the promise at the end of the day and observe what the experience of "hope" was like. Then talk to you children about what people were experiencing as they "hoped" for a king.

DAY THREE

What did God promise?

When Israel was a child, I loved him, and out of Egypt I called my son.

Hosea 11:1

Hosea was a very interesting prophet. He lived around the same time as Isaiah in the later part of the seventh century BC. Hosea carried God's words of warning to the northern kingdom of Israel. His message through the whole book helped people understand how their behavior was like a broken marriage—even though God stayed faithful, his "bride" was always leaving him. In the later part of the book, he used the analogy of a parent raising a child from infancy. While the child thought that it was all on its own, it was really the "parent" who was taking care of him and making sure that he was fed well and was safe. In the above verse, God is reminding the people that what motivated Him to call His people out of Egypt was his tremendous love—the love of a wonderful parent.

What did Matthew tell us?

Now when they had departed, behold, an angel of the Lord appeared to Joseph in a dream and said, "Rise, take the child and his mother, and flee to Egypt, and remain there until I tell you, for Herod is about to search for the child, to destroy him." And he rose and took the child and his mother by night and departed to Egypt and remained there until the death of Herod. This was to fulfill what the Lord had spoken by the prophet, "Out of Egypt I called my son."

Matthew 2:13–15

Matthew had recognized that the prophecy of God calling his Son out of Egypt wasn't just a "story" that Hosea told. It was a real prophecy of how God, the Father, loves his Son and protects him as a good parent would when Herod wanted to kill Jesus as a baby. When the angel told Joseph to take Jesus to Egypt, he was helping them escape from the land that Herod ruled and providing the protection that Joseph, Mary, and Jesus needed at the time.

Some things to discuss

When Matthew regards Jesus as God's Son, what do you think he wants you to know?

What emotions do you think God, the Father, has for His Son?

Ideas for parents: Ask your child to get his/her stuffed animal and talk about how it needs to be taken care of. When Jesus became a child, He needed to be taken care of. Why do you think Jesus was willing to become a child and need to be taken care of?

DAY FOUR

What did God promise?

"Hear the word of the Lord, O nations, and declare it in the coastlands far away; say, 'He who scattered Israel will gather him, and will keep him as a shepherd keeps his flock.' For the Lord has ransomed Jacob and has redeemed him from hands too strong for him. They shall come and sing aloud on the height of Zion, and they shall be radiant over the goodness of the Lord, over the grain, the wine, and the oil, and over the young of the flock and the herd; their life shall be like a watered garden, and they shall languish no more. Then shall the young women rejoice in the dance, and the young men and the old shall be merry. I will turn their mourning into joy; I will comfort them, and give them gladness for sorrow. I will feast the soul of the priests with abundance, and my people shall be satisfied with my goodness, declares the Lord." Thus says the Lord: "A voice is heard in Ramah, lamentation and bitter weeping. Rachel is weeping for her children; she refuses to be comforted for her children, because they are no more." Thus says the Lord: "Keep your voice from weeping, and your eyes from tears, for there is a reward for your work, declares the Lord, and they shall come back from the land of the enemy. There is hope for your future, declares the Lord, and your children shall come back to their own country.

Jeremiah 31: 10–17

Jeremiah was a prophet who had come to Israel after the prophets at whom we have looked thus far. All those prophets warned about the coming Assyrians, who would conquer the northern tribes of Israel (which happened in 722 BC). Jeremiah came about 100 years later when Babylon was rising as a world power. It was foretold, which later came true, that Babylon would eventually defeat Assyria, would take over the northern kingdom of Israel, and then would eventually invade Jerusalem and destroy the holy temple there (586 BC). Jeremiah had warned about Babylon and was alive when the Babylonians conquered Jerusalem and enslaved the nation.

In this message, Jeremiah is telling the people that one day they will be gathered back together out of enslavement they were dealing with at that time. It is a message of hope. We see the prophet describing the One who saves them as a shepherd who takes care of sheep who can't take care of themselves. Most of Jeremiah's message is hopeful and optimistic—except for one part. Part of the story tells about the sorrow over the loss of children. The words Jeremiah uses are common to the people of Israel, but it might help to lay out some reminders:

- This message is to a small group of people who had survived very tough days. They were a remnant of the whole nation.

- Ramah is a small town, just a bit north of Jerusalem. The people were captured on the route that they followed and were exiled to Babylon.

- The mothers are weeping because their children are no more. God's message to them is that even though their times are very tough, someday the "kids" would come back to the nation and people of Israel—so they should try and have hope amid their tears and grief.

Jeremiah wanted the people to know that even though their day-to-day lives had some very difficult problems, there was a reason to hope.

What did Matthew tell us?

Then Herod, when he saw that he had been tricked by the wise men, became furious, and he sent and killed all the male children in Bethlehem and in all that region who were two years old or under, according to the time that he had ascertained from the wise men. Then was fulfilled what was spoken by the prophet Jeremiah: "A voice was heard in Ramah, weeping and loud lamentation, Rachel weeping for her children; she refused to be comforted, because they are no more."

Matthew 2:16–18

We often like to think about the warm and fuzzy events that surrounded Jesus' birth, but there were challenges as well. Jesus' life was filled with these challenges.

Some things to discuss

In our study today, we see that some families lost babies whom they loved. How would you feel if that happened to you?

What do you need to stay hopeful for good things in the future while you go through hard times in the present?

Ideas for parents: Play (and maybe sing and dance together!!) "As the World Shakes." Talk about what it means to trust God, no matter what.

LEG ONE—HE ARRIVES!

What did Matthew want us to understand about this part of Jesus' life? In Leg One of this journey, we can see the amazing, miraculous events that occurred around Jesus' birth. Although he was born in a manger, he was no ordinary child!

His birth involved God's special grace on Mary so that Jesus could be both a man and the Son of God that he always was. His first audience were shepherds—which was so fitting because he was prophesized to be the Shepherd-King of Israel.

He was also protected by his Father in heaven. The local authorities that were threatened by his potential power tried, in vain, to end his life. He was even guided to a foreign country where he was safe and protected as a young baby.

He arrives, and we can see that this is a special person.

Leg Two—He Has a Message

DAY FIVE

What did God promise?

Comfort, comfort my people, says your God. Speak tenderly to Jerusalem, and cry to her that her warfare is ended, that her iniquity is pardoned, that she has received from the Lord's hand double for all her sins. A voice cries: "In the wilderness prepare the way of the Lord; make straight in the desert a highway for our God. Every valley shall be lifted up, and every mountain and hill be made low; the uneven ground shall become level, and the rough places a plain. And the glory of the Lord shall be revealed, and all flesh shall see it together, for the mouth of the Lord has spoken."

Isaiah 40:1–5

This passage is a big turning point in the book of Isaiah. His peers were captives in Babylon, and they deeply missed being in their own country. Isaiah's message to them was to take comfort in the present because a time would come when they would be able to return home.

Being rescued from slavery would not be a small event, someone special was going to come and tell them that they need to get ready and be prepared to return home - a very long journey. So, when Isaiah tells them that the ground will be leveled, he means that the Lord will make it a smooth journey for them, despite all the obstacles.

They didn't have much hope for fixing the tough situation in which they were. They needed to be rescued by the Lord and they would need to see his glory restored.

What did Matthew tell us?

In those days John the Baptist came preaching in the wilderness of Judea, "Repent, for the kingdom of heaven is at hand." For this is he who was spoken of by the prophet Isaiah when he said, "The voice of one crying in the wilderness: 'Prepare the way of the Lord; make his paths straight.'

Then Jesus came from Galilee to the Jordan to John, to be baptized by him. John would have prevented him, saying, "I need to be baptized by you, and do you come to me?" But Jesus answered him, "Let it be so now, for thus it is fitting for us to fulfill all righteousness." Then he consented. And when Jesus was baptized, immediately he went up from the water, and behold, the heavens were opened to him, and he saw the Spirit of God descending like a dove and coming to rest on him; and behold, a voice from heaven said, "This is my beloved Son, with whom I am well pleased."

Matthew 3:1–3 and 13–17

This passage of Matthew introduces a new word—kingdom. For the people of Israel, that usually meant a physical kingdom and a personal king, who decreed laws that had to be obeyed. Whoever had "their person" as king oversaw the government and controlled daily rules of living. Israel remembered what it was like when David was the king, and they always dreamt that those should come back. In fact, it was more than a dream since God had promised that they would have a king, like David, who will rule their nation. This promise was made all the way back at the time of Moses.

John the Baptist was preparing the nation for a new "king," but Jesus was going to be a different king and bring a kingdom different than the one that they were expecting. This story will develop more as we go along in our study.

Some things to discuss

When you think about celebrating Christmas, what are a few things that you can do to get prepared?

The people of Matthew's time wanted their problems to go away, and they thought that having their own king would be an important piece of the puzzle. What would you like to see different in your life that you think would help the difficulties that you face go away?

Why do you think God, the Father, sent the dove and shared his thoughts when Jesus was baptized?

Ideas for parents: Let your children pretend to be "king or queen" for an hour and observe what they would order to be done. Talk about the responsibility of being in charge and what one needs to do to be a good queen. Then talk about how Jesus was a different kind of king from what the people expected.

DAY SIX

What did God promise?

But there will be no gloom for her (the people of Israel) who was in anguish. In the former time he (God) brought into contempt the land of Zebulun and the land of Naphtali, but in the latter time he has made glorious the way of the sea, the land beyond the Jordan, Galilee of the nations. The people who walked in darkness have seen a great light; those who dwelt in a land of deep darkness, on them has light shone.

Behold my servant, whom I uphold, my chosen, in whom my soul delights; I have put my Spirit upon him; he will bring forth justice to the nations. He will not cry aloud or lift up his voice, or make it heard in the street; a bruised reed he will not break, and a faintly burning wick he will not quench; he will faithfully bring forth justice. He will not grow faint or be discouraged till he has established justice in the earth; and the coastlands wait for his law. Thus says God, the Lord, who created the heavens and stretched them out, who spread out the earth and what comes from it, who gives breath to the people on it and spirit to those who walk in it: I am the Lord; I have called you in righteousness; I will take you by the hand and keep you; I will give you as a covenant for the people, a light for the nations, to open the eyes that are blind, to bring out the prisoners from the dungeon, from the prison those who sit in darkness.

Isaiah 9:1–2 and 42:1–7

We need a small geography discussion to understand this passage. For the people of Israel, the northern part of the country had two problems. First, they set up their own kingdom that was separate from the capital city of Jerusalem where the temple to meet with God was located. Second, when enemies came to attack Israel, they came to the northern part of Israel first by following the land called the "fertile crescent". This route offered water and food that the armies of enemies needed. So, in Israel's history, the northern part of the country was often the first to fall prey to the attacking enemies. For these reasons it was considered a "lesser" part of the country. Zebulun and Naphtali were the two tribes that occupied the northern part of Israel. Isaiah is telling them that the king that they all wanted to have would come from that northern part of the country. That was quite unexpected given the reputation of northern part of the country in their culture.

Isaiah also said that the coming king and kingdom would bring "light." The second passage from Isaiah explains more about what it means to bring light. The idea was that injustice can happen when people can't see or understand all that is going on. The "covering up" of evil and injustice is what allows it to exist. The new king would bring light that will expose all evil, and hence allow the return of justice.

What did Matthew tell us?

Now when he heard that John had been arrested, he withdrew into Galilee. And leaving Nazareth he went and lived in Capernaum by the sea, in the territory of Zebulun and Naphtali, so that what was spoken by the prophet Isaiah might be fulfilled: The land of Zebulun and the land of Naphtali, the way of the sea, beyond the Jordan, Galilee of the Gentiles—the people dwelling in darkness have seen a

great light, and for those dwelling in the region and shadow
of death, on them a light has dawned." From that time Jesus
began to preach, saying, "Repent, for the kingdom of heaven
is at hand."

Matthew 4:12–17

Here we can see why this is important to Matthew. The people had gotten very accustomed to all the important and powerful people being from Jerusalem. Jesus started his ministry on earth in the northern part of Israel, which might have seemed both unexpected and unhealthy to the powerful people at the time of Jesus. Matthew wanted them to remember what Isaiah had foretold.

Jesus' message to the people "up north" was a call for repentance. This was the starting point for people to go from where they were at, to now enter the coming kingdom and experience that "great light". The presence of the kingdom of heaven, the source of that light, had now come.

Some things to discuss

Even in our everyday life, where you are from can make a big difference in how people think of you and treat you. Do you think where you are from matters to God?

Jesus starts his message with the word, "repent." What does "repent" mean to you?

Ideas for parents: Set up an obstacle course, turn out the lights and have the kids navigate through the room. Then have them repeat the course with a flashlight in hand. Talk about what it is like to have enough light to see the next step.

DAY SEVEN

What did God promise?

Who has believed what he has heard from us? And to whom has the arm of the Lord been revealed? For he grew up before him like a young plant, and like a root out of dry ground; he had no form or majesty that we should look at him, and no beauty that we should desire him. He was despised and rejected by men, a man of sorrows and acquainted with grief; and as one from whom men hide their faces he was despised, and we esteemed him not.

Surely he has borne our griefs and carried our sorrows; yet we esteemed him stricken, smitten by God, and afflicted. But he was pierced for our transgressions; he was crushed for our iniquities; upon him was the chastisement that brought us peace, and with his wounds we are healed. All we like sheep have gone astray; we have turned—every one—to his own way; and the Lord has laid on him the iniquity of us all.

Isaiah 53:1–6

In the closing section of the book of Isaiah, the prophet has a message of hope for the suffering people. While they fully deserved all that they were dealing with, in the end, God would be faithful to his promise to Abraham—that the whole world would be blessed through the descendants of Israel. Isaiah wanted not only to remind them of God's faithfulness, but also urge them to see how much God was sacrificing to redeem and restore his people.

The Messiah would be the bearer of all the terrible consequences of our sin. That burden would cover many things, one of which was the physical suffering that people bear because of sin. And as he would bear that burden, he would be rejected and despised by those he was rescuing.

What did Matthew tell us?

And when Jesus entered Peter's house, he saw his mother-in-law lying sick with a fever. He touched her hand, and the fever left her, and she rose and began to serve him. That evening they brought to him many who were oppressed by demons, and he cast out the spirits with a word and healed all who were sick. This was to fulfill what was spoken by the prophet Isaiah: "He took our illnesses and bore our diseases."

Matthew 8:14–17

An important part of what Matthew wants us to know is that Jesus was not only fulfilling prophecies, but he was also displaying his uniquely powerful strengths! Jesus wasn't just a normal person who had some good things to say, he also had the power to heal people in ways that no other person could.

Some things to discuss

Why do you think Jesus took so much time to heal people?

What does Jesus' decision to help tell you about Jesus? As you think about this topic, one piece of history might help. Back in Jesus' day, the most common way sick people were treated was to send them away and not let them be near healthy people. They didn't have ways to protect the caregivers from contracting the diseases with which people were struggling, so rather than taking them in to give them help, they sent them away until they either got better or died. It was a big deal for Jesus to touch and heal so many people who were sick. Jesus bore more than just their sicknesses.

We will talk more about this in days to come as Matthew tells the whole story.

DAY EIGHT

What did God promise?

What shall I do with you, O Ephraim? What shall I do with you, O Judah? Your love is like a morning cloud, like the dew that goes early away. Therefore I have hewn them by the prophets; I have slain them by the words of my mouth, and my judgment goes forth as the light. For I desire steadfast love and not sacrifice, the knowledge of God rather than burnt offerings.

Hosea 6:4–6

This is our second visit with Hosea. In this message, Hosea was trying to help the people see the need to have a deep relationship with God, not just one on the surface. It was a priority for the people of Hosea's time to go through some of their religious practices by just following the rules and not really connecting their hearts and souls to God. They wanted to do enough to make it look like they were obeying the rules that God wanted them to follow, without really loving God. Hosea compared it to morning dew—it looks like the water was there to nourish the plants, but as soon as a little heat showed up, it evaporated and was gone.

As important as the law was, it was nothing compared to the importance of having a heart full of real love for God and a deep desire to have a personal relationship with him—not just going through the motions of offering sacrifices.

What did Matthew tell us?

As Jesus passed on from there, he saw a man called Matthew sitting at the tax booth, and he said to him, "Follow me." And he rose and followed him.

And as Jesus reclined at table in the house, behold, many tax collectors and sinners came and were reclining with Jesus and his disciples. And when the Pharisees saw this, they said to his disciples, "Why does your teacher eat with tax collectors and sinners?" But when he heard it, he said, "Those who are well have no need of a physician, but those who are sick. Go and learn what this means: 'I desire mercy, and not sacrifice.' For I came not to call the righteous, but sinners."

Matthew 9:9–13

To understand this passage, we need to know who a tax collector was. The people of Israel had been conquered by Rome and they had to pay very high taxes. Romans hired Jewish people to collect those high taxes and send them back to Rome. These tax collectors got rich doing this job, but the Jewish people hated them because they were seen as traitors.

Jesus built a relationship with one of these hated tax collectors and not only did he invite Matthew to be a disciple, he also went to his house for dinner. The Pharisees thought that Jesus was "breaking a rule" by being connected with these hated people, and they wanted to understand how Jesus, a teacher to whom many people had started to listen to, could make this decision.

Jesus quotes from Hosea to teach two lessons. First, God loves everyone—including tax collectors—and wants them to be in a relationship with him. Second, the Pharisees are going through the motions, but their hearts are struggling just like the leaders of Hosea's day—they went through those motions without really having a heart of love for God or for the people that God loves.

Some things to discuss

How would you describe the difference between "just following the rules" and really loving God?

Matthew decided to follow Jesus, and, later in his life, he wrote the book that we are studying today! When you think about your own choices and priorities in your day-to-day decision making, what helps you to be one who follows Jesus?

DAY NINE

What did God promise?

Moses spoke to the Lord, saying, "Let the Lord, the God of the spirits of all flesh, appoint a man over the congregation who shall go out before them and come in before them, who shall lead them out and bring them in, that the congregation of the Lord may not be as sheep that have no shepherd.

Numbers 27:15–17

And he shall stand and shepherd his flock in the strength of the Lord, in the majesty of the name of the Lord his God. And they shall dwell secure, for now he shall be great to the ends of the earth.

Micah 5:4

The prophets of the Old Testament frequently used the picture of sheep and a shepherd to talk about their situation. The key to this metaphor is that the sheep need someone to lead them, because they wander and cannot survive when left on their own. The stronger and wiser the shepherd, the better it is for the sheep.

What did Matthew tell us?

And Jesus went throughout all the cities and villages, teaching in their synagogues and proclaiming the gospel of the kingdom and healing every disease and every affliction. When he saw the crowds, he had compassion for them, because they were harassed and helpless, like sheep without a shepherd. Then he said to His disciples, "The harvest is plentiful, but the laborers are few; therefore pray earnestly to the Lord of the harvest to send out laborers into his harvest."

Matthew 9:35–38

At the time when Jesus was here on earth, the people he was trying to care for did not have good leadership. Every day Jesus was faced with people who had huge needs and struggles, and who needed help. Jesus reminded the people about the prophets who spoke of a coming shepherd who would lead the people well.

Some things to discuss

Often at Christmastime we see sheep around the manger. The Bible is full of references to sheep and their need of a shepherd. Why do we need a good shepherd?

What are some ways in which you need Jesus to take the lead in your life?

LEG TWO—HE HAS A MESSAGE

What did Matthew want us to understand about this part of Jesus' life? In Leg Two we see the introduction of Jesus as an adult to the people of Israel. They had been, for a very long time, enslaved by other nations. They wanted to be free and have their own king, just like they had King David about a thousand years earlier. Jesus and John the Baptist both went all over the country telling people that the promised king had come, and that the kingdom would be re-established.

There are some twists in the story because how Jesus lived was unexpected. He hung out with people who were rejected by the Jewish leaders but didn't hang out in the capital city of the country— Jerusalem. It didn't seem to fit what others were expecting; however, he was able to do all sorts of miracles, and his heart was "all in" in wanting to bring good news to everyone.

In Leg Two we see the proposal—this is the king, and he will re-establish the kingdom. But something about how the people are responding doesn't feel quite right.

Leg Three—He's Different than Expected

DAY TEN

What did God promise?

Before we start, today's study needs a bit of explaining! We have been looking back and comparing what was promised with what actually happened in Jesus' life. In this passage Jesus is doing the same "look back" with John the Baptist! John had told everyone that Jesus was the promised Messiah, but then he ended up in prison and wasn't so sure that Jesus was going to deliver what John thought was going to happen. So, he asked Jesus," Are you really the One?"

In response, Jesus gave a list of examples where what he had done was what had been prophesied by the other prophets as evidence that he really is the promised Messiah. Let's jump in and then sort it out when we get to Jesus' discussion.

Behold, I send my messenger, and he will prepare the way
before me. And the Lord whom you seek will suddenly come

to his temple; and the messenger of the covenant in whom you delight, behold, he is coming, says the Lord of hosts.

Malachi 3:1

Your dead shall live; their bodies shall rise. You who dwell in the dust, awake and sing for joy! For your dew is a dew of light, and the earth will give birth to the dead.

Isaiah 26:19

In that day the deaf shall hear the words of a book, and out of their gloom and darkness the eyes of the blind shall see.

Isaiah 29:18

Then the eyes of the blind shall be opened, and the ears of the deaf unstopped; then shall the lame man leap like a deer, and the tongue of the mute sing for joy.

Isaiah 35:5–6

The Spirit of the Lord God is upon me, because the Lord has anointed me to bring good news to the poor; he has sent me to bind up the brokenhearted, to proclaim liberty to the captives, and the opening of the prison to those who are bound.

Isaiah 61:1

What did Matthew tell us?

Now when John heard in prison about the deeds of the Christ, he sent word by his disciples and said to him, "Are you the one who is to come, or shall we look for another?" And Jesus answered them, "Go and tell John what you hear and see:

- *the blind receive their sight (Is 29:18, 35:5)*

- *the lame walk, lepers are cleansed (Is 35:6)*

- *the deaf hear, (Is 29:18–19, 35:5)*

- *the dead are raised up (Is 26:18–19),*

- *the poor have good news preached to them (Is 61:1).*

- *And blessed is the one who is not offended by me."*

As they went away, Jesus began to speak to the crowds concerning John: "What did you go out into the wilderness to see? A reed shaken by the wind? What then did you go out to see? A man dressed in soft clothing? Behold, those who wear soft clothing are in kings' houses. What then did you go out to see? A prophet? Yes, I tell you, and more than a prophet. This is he of whom it is written, Behold, I send my messenger before your face, who will prepare your way before you."

Truly, I say to you, among those born of women there has arisen no one greater than John the Baptist. Yet the one who is least in the kingdom of heaven is greater than he. From the days of John the Baptist until now the kingdom of heaven has suffered violence, and the violent take it by force. For all the Prophets and the Law prophesied until John, and if you are willing to accept it, he is Elijah who is to come. He who has ears to hear, let him hear.

Matthew 11:2–15

Can you see what John was wondering about and how Jesus answered him? Jesus gave John some facts that confirmed that what he was doing was the same as that the prophets from the past had said the

Messiah would do. But Jesus didn't stop there! He went on to explain to those around him that John had fulfilled prophecy from the past as one who would prepare the people. But now, with Jesus here, how people connect with God will be very different than how it was for all the past prophets up to John.

Some things to discuss

Does it make a difference to you that Jesus took time to share some "facts" about his life that showed he did what the prophets promised?

The prophets were very important people to the nation of Israel since God spoke through them. Jesus is explaining that now that he has come, how we connect with God and hear him has changed. What is it that Jesus brought that is new?

Ideas for parents: Does someone in your family wear glasses? Ask that person to take off the glasses and share them with someone who doesn't wear them. Ask from everyone, "What do you see?" For those who need glasses, talk about what it was like when they first got glasses and could see clearly. Jesus was helping people see what had always been blurry.

DAY ELEVEN

What did God promise?

*Behold my servant, whom I uphold, my chosen, in whom my
soul delights; I have put my Spirit upon him; he will bring
forth justice to the nations. He will not cry aloud or lift up
his voice, or make it heard in the street; a bruised reed he
will not break, and a faintly burning wick he will not quench;
he will faithfully bring forth justice.*

Isaiah 42: 1–3

This passage is part of a larger group of passages that span Isaiah
40–52. This section of Isaiah includes four "Servant Songs" where
different attributes of the Messiah as a servant are framed. This is an
unexpected description of a person who would bring about justice to
all nations and was referred to as a king. Israel was captive to a mighty
opponent, and Isaiah was telling them that the one who would bring
the justice they felt they deserved would be a tender servant.

What did Matthew tell us?

*But the Pharisees went out and conspired against him, how
to destroy him.*

*Jesus, aware of this, withdrew from there. And many fol-
lowed him, and he healed them all and ordered them not
to make him known. This was to fulfill what was spoken
by the prophet Isaiah: "Behold, my servant whom I have
chosen, my beloved with whom my soul is well pleased. I
will put my Spirit upon him, and he will proclaim justice
to the Gentiles. He will not quarrel or cry aloud, nor will*

anyone hear his voice in the streets; a bruised reed he will not break, until he brings justice to victory; and in his name the Gentiles will hope."

Matthew 12:14–21

It's important to understand the picture that Matthew was trying to paint. The one he believed was the Savior was quickly becoming an arch enemy of the powerful, "religious" Pharisees who not only disagreed with his teaching but also wanted to kill him!

You might have expected Jesus to haul off and attack those Pharisees, but he pulls away instead, effectively hiding from the Pharisees. And as he healed people, he asked them not to let the Pharisees figure out where he was. This humble position that Jesus took was exactly what Isaiah was talking about, and Matthew wanted everyone to see the connection.

Some things to discuss

Why do you think that Jesus' example of being a humble servant was hard for people to accept?

Why do you think the Pharisees wanted to kill Jesus?

What is special about Jesus that makes him one in whom we can all hope?

DAY TWELVE

What did God promise?

*And I heard the voice of the Lord saying, "Whom shall I
send, and who will go for us?" Then I said, "Here I am! Send
me." And he said, "Go, and say to this people: "''Keep on
hearing, but do not understand; keep on seeing, but do not
perceive.' Make the heart of this people dull, and their ears
heavy, and blind their eyes; lest they see with their eyes, and
hear with their ears, and understand with their hearts, and
turn and be healed.*

Isaiah 6:9–10

This is the calling by the Lord for Isaiah to be a prophet. And what
a job description it was—go, work very hard, and no one will listen!

As Isaiah took his message to the people, he was met with many
who didn't "hear" what he had to say. The Lord prepped Isaiah by let-
ting him know that people have a hard time changing their ways and
often cannot listen when what they are being told means they need
to change something about the choices they make.

What did Matthew tell us?

*Then the disciples came and said to him, "Why do you speak
to them in parables?" And he answered them, "To you it has
been given to know the secrets of the kingdom of heaven, but
to them it has not been given. For to the one who has, more
will be given, and he will have an abundance, but from the
one who has not, even what he has will be taken away. This*

is why I speak to them in parables, because seeing they do not see, and hearing they do not hear, nor do they understand. Indeed, in their case the prophecy of Isaiah is fulfilled that says: "'You will indeed hear but never understand, and you will indeed see but never perceive.' For this people's heart has grown dull, and with their ears they can barely hear, and their eyes they have closed, lest they should see with their eyes and hear with their ears and understand with their heart and turn, and I would heal them."

But blessed are your eyes, for they see, and your ears, for they hear. For truly, I say to you, many prophets and righteous people longed to see what you see, and did not see it, and to hear what you hear, and did not hear it.

Matthew 13:10–17

This is really a great question. Jesus usually spoke in parables, and as the disciples were watching, they could tell that many were not getting the message. So the disciples asked, "Jesus, if you want to change their minds, why can't you just be clear and direct?"

Jesus underscored how amazing this period was compared to Israel's history. The disciples were "getting it" because the Spirit of God was helping them understand the prophets of old and the parables that Jesus told. And what they were getting were the secrets to what the kingdom of heaven is really like. We will study this "kingdom" more but skipping ahead a bit for now—the Kingdom that Jesus brought was way different than what the people wanted and what they were expecting. Those "wants and expectations" were blocking their ability to see and hear what Jesus was telling them.

Some things to discuss

What can make it hard for us to hear what God is telling us?

Given what you have read and discussed so far, what kind of kingdom was Jesus bringing?

Ideas for parents: Before jumping into the questions, try asking this from your kids: How many times have you been told to clean your room or brush your teeth? What made it hard to remember that you had to get those things done?

DAY THIRTEEN

What did God promise?

The Spirit of the Lord God is upon me, because the Lord has anointed me to bring good news to the poor; he has sent me to bind up the brokenhearted, to proclaim liberty to the captives, and the opening of the prison to those who are bound; to proclaim the year of the Lord's favor; and the day of vengeance of our God; to comfort all who mourn; to grant to those who mourn in Zion—to give them a beautiful headdress instead of ashes, the oil of gladness instead of mourning, the garment of praise instead of a faint spirit; that they may be called oaks of righteousness, the planting of the Lord, that he may be glorified.

Isaiah 61: 1–3

In ancient Israel there was a provision in the Law which was called "The Year of the Lord's Favor" or the "Year of Jubilee." This was a time that was supposed to be celebrated every fifty years. It was to make sure, in a structured way, that things were in balance in the nation of Israel. In the day-to-day working of life, some things that are unfair may develop. For example, some people might own large pieces of land and other families are homeless. As humans, we are not perfect, and as a result things may happen that may not be in the best interest for everyone. The Year of the Lord's Favor was a year to fix such imbalances, where people who had too much gave up some of their wealth and property to those who didn't have enough. It was intended to get things back in balance in the way it was when it first got established under Moses and Joshua.

Isaiah was speaking to a group of people who had lost all their property and whose culture had become a mess. God's Spirit told Isaiah to tell the people that in the future a year would come to fix all imbalances, and that the Messiah would deliver it and get the nation back to what they had under King David.

What did Matthew (and Luke!) tell us?

And when Jesus had finished these parables, he went away from there, and coming to his hometown he taught them in their synagogue, so that they were astonished, and said, "Where did this man get this wisdom and these mighty works?

Matthew 13:53–54

And he came to Nazareth, where he had been brought up. And as was his custom, he went to the synagogue on the Sabbath day, and he stood up to read. And the scroll of the prophet Isaiah was given to him. He unrolled the scroll and found the place where it was written, "The Spirit of the Lord is upon me, because he has anointed me to proclaim good news to the poor. He has sent me to proclaim liberty to the captives and recovering of sight to the blind, to set at liberty those who are oppressed, to proclaim the year of the Lord's favor."

And he rolled up the scroll and gave it back to the attendant and sat down. And the eyes of all in the synagogue were fixed on him. And he began to say to them, "Today this Scripture has been fulfilled in your hearing.

Luke 4:16–21

This is another very big deal in our story. Let's try and put ourselves in the shoes of the people to whom Jesus was speaking in the synagogue.

First, Jesus was back in his hometown. This is where Jesus grew up. The people who were gathered that day in church (synagogue was their church) remembered Jesus as a kid when Mary and Joseph raised him and his brothers.

Second, this passage that he read from in Isaiah was one of the most important passages from Isaiah to the people who were listening. This was a promise that God had made to the people of Israel that a day will come when the Messiah would "fix" everything. And Jesus read that passage and said— "I am the one who is here to fix everything." Remember—the people who were listening felt like everything was still broken because the nation of Rome was ruling over them, and they were not able to function the way they wanted to. They needed things to get "fixed" as Isaiah had promised

So, Matthew wants us to see and understand the dilemma that these people had—Jesus, the guy they had seen grow up among them, thinks he is the one who is going to overthrow Rome and get everything back to the way it was under King David. Really?

Third, this is a big change for Jesus. Remember how we saw that Jesus had been speaking to people in parables? He is taking a step in a different direction now by clearly, and in very direct language, proclaiming that he is the Messiah whom Isaiah had said would come. It was a new day in the life of Jesus.

Some things to discuss

If you heard someone say that they were here to "fix everything," what would you expect that person to be like?

The most powerful people in the days of Jesus came from the center of their nation—Jerusalem. Jesus grew up in the northern part of Israel, in an area that was famous for fishermen, not for powerful people. Would it have been hard for you to think that a carpenter from a small town could fix everything?

DAY FOURTEEN

What did God promise?

And the Lord said: "Because this people draw near with their
mouth and honor me with their lips, while their hearts are
far from me, and their fear of me is a commandment taught
by men, therefore, behold, I will again do wonderful things
with this people, with wonder upon wonder; and the wisdom
of their wise men shall perish, and the discernment of their
discerning men shall be hidden."

Isaiah 29:13–14

This is the part of Isaiah's life where he was warning the people about
their bad behavior. He saw people who, on the outside, pretended like
they were devoted to keeping the law and pursuing what was right
before God, whereas, on the inside, they were only interested in pursuing what they wanted for themselves. They considered themselves
to be wise and discerning, but it wasn't real. And Isaiah was telling
them that eventually God's goodness would prevail, and the people will
experience a wonderful God when these bad leaders are pushed aside.

What did Matthew tell us?

Then Pharisees and scribes came to Jesus from Jerusalem
and said, "Why do your disciples break the tradition of the
elders? For they do not wash their hands when they eat." He
answered them, "And why do you break the commandment
of God for the sake of your tradition?" For God commanded,
"Honor your father and our mother," and, "Whoever reviles
father or mother must surely die." But you say, "If anyone

tells his father or his mother, 'What you would have gained from me is given to God,' he need not honor his father." So for the sake of your tradition you have made void the word of God. You hypocrites! Well did Isaiah prophesy of you, when he said: "This people honors me with their lips, but their heart is far from me; in vain do they worship me, teaching as doctrines the commandments of men."

Matthew 15:1–9

The Pharisees and scribes were the religious leaders during the time Jesus was on earth, and they lived and worked in Jerusalem. They heard more and more about Jesus, so they left Jerusalem and went up to Nazareth to see what this "Jesus thing" was all about.

The main way the Pharisees and scribes worked was to create rules that they said, on the outside, were intended to help obey God. But what was really happening, on the inside, was that these rules were designed to get them what they wanted. Jesus called them out as hypocrites—ones who say one thing but then do another.

The Pharisees had a rule about washing hands. Their intent was to appear as clean as possible when eating with other people like they would at mealtime. They were looking for a way to show that Jesus wasn't a rule follower, and they saw that he didn't wash his hands in the same way they did. So, they portrayed him as a rule breaker, which meant that he really couldn't be the Messiah he said he was.

Jesus called them out to show how fake their "rulemaking" was. God had asked the people to take care of their family members and to make sure that they had what they needed. The Pharisees made up some other rules that allowed them to promise their money to the "temple," and, if they did that, they could use it as part of their own wealth and not support their families. They kept that money rather than taking care of the needs of others. Jesus told the crowds that their rulemaking showed their truly bad intentions. They called themselves rule keepers, but in reality, they were figuring out how to break the intentions of the rules they didn't want to keep.

Some things to discuss

Jesus said some very harsh things to the people who were very powerful in his time. Why do you think he did that?

What do you think is the difference between just following rules and really believing something in your heart?

Ideas for parents: Have you kids talk about some of the rules around the house and ask them why those might be good rules. Then have them make up five silly rules and talk about whether it would be a good idea to follow those silly rules. Discuss the aspects that can be healthy or unhealthy about rules.

LEG THREE—
HE'S DIFFERENT THAN EXPECTED

What did Matthew want us to understand about this part of Jesus' life? In Leg Three Jesus tosses down an ultimatum—following me will be different than what the leaders thought it should be like. And this message frames two contrasting options:

> Option one: Listen to the ones who are in power and succumb to their authority and directions.

> Option two: Believe that a different sort of king is needed to deliver a message to those who have been suppressed and have suffered the most.

Digging deep into your heart is where you make a life-choice between these two options. And only those who are willing to follow Jesus will be able to understand what this new kingdom will be like.

Leg Four—He Is Rejected

DAY FIFTEEN

What did God promise?

Rejoice greatly, O daughter of Zion! Shout aloud, O daughter of Jerusalem! Behold, your king is coming to you; righteous and having salvation is he, humble and mounted on a donkey, on a colt, the foal of a donkey.

Zechariah 9:9

We get to meet a new prophet! Zechariah was a priest who served in the temple around 520 BC. This was a tough time for people who worked in the temple. They had been freed from Babylon and allowed to get back to Jerusalem. That was great news. They had started to rebuild things, but then they got stuck. Everyone was both frustrated and depressed that the kingdom did not seem to be returning to what it was under David.

Zechariah's message was that the promised kingdom would come, but it might be different than what was expected. In those days, when a king would enter the city that they had conquered in a battle, he would ride into the conquered city on a mighty military horse. The horse symbolized power. Zechariah was telling the people that this promised king would come, but in a manner of deep humility.

What did Matthew tell us?

Now when they drew near to Jerusalem and came to Bethphage, to the Mount of Olives, then Jesus sent two disciples, saying to them, "Go into the village in front of you, and immediately you will find a donkey tied, and a colt with her. Untie them and bring them to me. If anyone says anything to you, you shall say, 'The Lord needs them,' and he will send them at once." This took place to fulfill what was spoken by the prophet, saying, "Say to the daughter of Zion, 'Behold, your king is coming to you, humble, and mounted on a donkey, and on a colt, the foal of a beast of burden.'"

The disciples went and did as Jesus had directed them. They brought the donkey and the colt and put on them their cloaks, and he sat on them. Most of the crowd spread their cloaks on the road, and others cut branches from the trees and spread them on the road. And the crowds that went before him and that followed him were shouting, "Hosanna to the Son of David! Blessed is he who comes in the name of the Lord! Hosanna in the highest! And when he entered Jerusalem, the whole city was stirred up, saying, "Who is this?" And the crowds said, "This is the prophet Jesus, from Nazareth of Galilee."

Matthew 21:1–11

This is an amazing day in the life of Jesus. Crowds and crowds of people were anticipating that this person, Jesus, who had been up north, was finally arriving in Jerusalem. They were expecting that he would be setting up shop as the king. No higher honor could be bestowed on someone than to be called the Son of David. Everyone in Jerusalem believed that the king would come from the family line of David and would get things back to what they were like under David. When they saw Jesus on a colt, they remembered what Zechariah had said.

Some things to discuss

The people were willing to put their own clothes in the dirt so that Jesus would have a "clean ride in." What do you think they were hoping would happen?

Riding a colt instead of a war horse was sending a message that humility is important. As you think about what you have learned about Jesus so far, what are some ways in which you think we can be humble like he was?

DAY SIXTEEN

What did God promise?

A Psalm of David.

O Lord, our Lord, how majestic is your name in all the earth! You have set your glory above the heavens. Out of the mouth of babies and infants, you have established strength because of your foes, to still the enemy and the avenger.

Psalm 8:1–2

This was a song of celebration that David had written to praise God for his amazing work of creation. The song declares that God makes us and loves us. It is truly humbling to think about how great God is. Even the simplest, young children speak to the majesty of God.

What did Matthew tell us?

And the blind and the lame came to him in the temple, and he healed them. But when the chief priests and the scribes saw the wonderful things that he did, and the children crying out in the temple, "Hosanna to the Son of David!" they were indignant, and they said to him, "Do you hear what these are saying?" And Jesus said to them, "Yes; have you never read, 'Out of the mouth of infants and nursing babies you have prepared praise?" And leaving them, he went out of the city to Bethany and lodged there.

Matthew 21:14–17

In this part of his life, we have seen Jesus to be very bold in proclaiming who he was—the Son of God and the Messiah. This passage is an example of what was happening in Jerusalem.

For the Jewish people, the "Son of David" was the person who would restore the nation to what the kingdom was like under King David. And as the prophets talked about the coming of that Son of David, they helped the people understand that this coming king would be God himself. So, when the Pharisees heard the children proclaim that Jesus was the Son of David what everyone heard was that this Jesus, who was standing right in front of them in the city of Jerusalem, was THAT ONE. But because Jesus was so different than the expectations and ideas that the Pharisees had about the Messiah, they became angry when that title was used for Jesus.

They were asking Jesus to stop the children. Instead, he reminded the Pharisees of one of David's most popular psalms that predicted that the glory of the Son of David would be proclaimed by the mouths of young people. Jesus was saying, "I'm not going to stop them—they've got it right. And even more, you Pharisees are the ones who need to be stopped."

Some things to discuss

Sometimes we find it hard to say what we really feel and believe. Why do you think the young folks in this account were able to make such bold statements about Jesus?

What are some ways in which we can share with others what we think and feel about Jesus?

DAY SEVENTEEN

What did God promise?

Oh give thanks to the Lord, for he is good; for his steadfast love endures forever!

It is better to take refuge in the Lord than to trust in man. It is better to take refuge in the Lord than to trust in princes.

Open to me the gates of righteousness, that I may enter through them and give thanks to the Lord. This is the gate of the Lord; the righteous shall enter through it. I thank you that you have answered me and have become my salvation. The stone that the builders rejected has become the cornerstone. This is the Lord's doing; it is marvelous in our eyes. This is the day that the Lord has made; let us rejoice and be glad in it.

Psalm 118:1; 8–9; 19–24

This was a celebration psalm. Picture some large gates that were part of the entrance to the temple—the place where people would gather to meet with God. The Jewish people had been through great struggles in their history as a nation, but God had saved them. His love for them didn't flinch, leave, or get weaker even when they were disobedient. And now they could enter the Lord's presence not because people had a great building, but instead because the presence of God was based solely on God's work. He was a unique cornerstone that human builders didn't even think was useful for a building.

God's ways are different, but he always delivers on his promises because his steadfast love never goes away.

What did Matthew tell us?

Hear another parable. There was a master of a house who planted a vineyard and put a fence around it and dug a winepress in it and built a tower and leased it to tenants, and went into another country. When the season for fruit drew near, he sent his servants to the tenants to get his fruit. And the tenants took his servants and beat one, killed another, and stoned another. Again he sent other servants, more than the first. And they did the same to them. Finally he sent his son to them, saying, 'They will respect my son.' But when the tenants saw the son, they said to themselves, 'This is the heir. Come, let us kill him and have his inheritance.' And they took him and threw him out of the vineyard and killed him. When therefore the owner of the vineyard comes, what will he do to those tenants? They said to him, "He will put those wretches to a miserable death and let out the vineyard to other tenants who will give him the fruits in their seasons." Jesus said to them, "Have you never read in the Scriptures: 'The stone that the builders rejected has become the cornerstone; this was the Lord's doing, and it is marvelous in our eyes'?

Therefore I tell you, the kingdom of God will be taken away from you and given to a people producing its fruits. And the one who falls on this stone will be broken to pieces; and when it falls on anyone, it will crush him."

When the chief priests and the Pharisees heard his parables, they perceived that he was speaking about them. And although they were seeking to arrest him, they feared the crowds, because they held him to be a prophet.

Matthew 21:33–46

In this parable Jesus is making a very important point. As we have been seeing, the leaders of the people were rejecting Jesus as the promised king because he wasn't matching their expectations of what the king would be like. But Jesus could see inside their hearts and understand that their rejection of him was due to their selfishness and inability to let their power or influence be taken away. They wanted to keep the profits from the vineyard.

Jesus was making it very clear to them that because they were choosing to reject him as the king, the opportunity to be part of the kingdom was going to be given to other people. And those Pharisees and priests could see it coming, that if Jesus was going to get his way, they were going to lose all their power and wealth.

Some things to discuss

What is it in us that can make us selfish?

How does God want us to treat his Son whom he sent to be with us?

DAY EIGHTEEN

What did God promise?

In our advent journey, we are going to change direction a bit. So far, we have seen Matthew building a case to prove that Jesus was the long-promised Messiah, and that we should choose to follow him just like he did. But Matthew has more to tell us about what he learned from Jesus.

What we want to look at now is our response to this key question: If Jesus is the one whom God had sent to rescue us, what should we do?

What did Matthew tell us?

Now when Jesus came into the district of Caesarea Philippi, he asked his disciples, "Who do people say that the Son of Man is?" And they said, "Some say John the Baptist, others say Elijah, and others Jeremiah or one of the prophets. He said to them, "But who do you say that I am?" Simon Peter replied, "You are the Christ, the Son of the living God." And Jesus answered him, "Blessed are you, Simon Bar-Jonah! For flesh and blood has not revealed this to you, but my Father who is in heaven. And I tell you, you are Peter, and on this rock I will build my church, and the gates of hell shall not prevail against it. I will give you the keys of the kingdom of heaven, and whatever you bind on earth shall be bound in heaven, and whatever you loose on earth shall be loosed in heaven. Then he strictly charged the disciples to tell no one that he was the Christ.

Matthew 16:13–20

The people who were following Jesus had seen a lot of miracles. They had seen Jesus enable blind people to see, paralyzed people to walk, sick people who had no chance of getting better be healed and dead people come back to life. They had seen Jesus deal with harsh political enemies, stand up for the truth, and win arguments. They had seen him walk on water showing his power over nature. And Jesus knew that the crowds were trying to find an answer to this question: Who is this Jesus? Could he really be the promised one about whom Isaiah spoke over 750 years ago, the one who will fix all their problems with Rome, and the one who will get them back to the way things were in King David's kingdom?

Jesus knew that everyone was wondering about him, and he wanted to hear what his closest disciples thought.

When Peter answered with "the Christ," he was using a word that meant that Jesus was the Messiah—the one who had come to rescue them. That meant that he was God himself, who had come as a man. When Jesus heard Peter's response, he lit up and made sure that they understood that figuring that out wasn't like solving a math problem with good logic, but instead was a gift that God had given to them now, to be used to change the world.

Some things to discuss

Do you think that Jesus did enough things to prove that he was the Son of God?

From what you have seen so far in Jesus' walk, does he seem like a kind of person who can establish the kingdom of heaven on this planet?

There is a terrific video produced by the Bible Project that describes the Kingdom of God. It can be found at bibleproject.com It is entitled, "Gospel of the Kingdom".

Enjoy!

DAY NINETEEN
What did Matthew tell us?

Then Jesus told his disciples, "If anyone would come after me, let him deny himself and take up his cross and follow me. For whoever would save his life will lose it, but whoever loses his life for my sake will find it. For what will it profit a man if he gains the whole world and forfeits his soul? Or what shall a man give in return for his soul? For the Son of Man is going to come with his angels in the glory of his Father, and then he will repay each person according to what he has done. Truly, I say to you, there are some standing here who will not taste death until they see the Son of Man coming in his kingdom.

Matthew 16:24–28

Jesus asked the question: "Who do you say I am?" And Jesus loved Peter's answer. But now Jesus must tell them something that is very important and unexpected.

Jesus explained that he was the Messiah, the Savior. It would be normal to think that good days were coming. That finally Jesus would fix everything broken in their world. That he would step up and take over running the country so that this could be the kind of nation of which the people had been dreaming. That they could have the best possible life. But having said that he, instead, calls them to follow him—not to a throne but to a cross.

In those days, if Romans, who oversaw running the country, thought that someone was trying to take back his/her country, they punished that person in a way that would make everyone afraid to ever attempt to overthrow them as rulers. They nailed the persons' body to a cross in public and let the person stay on that cross until they died. Jesus was telling his disciples that following him as the Messiah was the same as deciding to be nailed to a cross.

Some things to discuss

It would be easy to say "I want to follow Jesus" if following him meant that he would grant all your wishes. Is that what Jesus promised?

It can be hard to accept Jesus as the Messiah and to choose to follow him since a journey with him might be difficult. How do you make that sort of choice?

LEG FOUR—HE IS REJECTED

What did Matthew want us to see about this part of Jesus' life? In Leg Four, everyone around Jesus was called to decide— "Who do you say that I am?"

- Some were afraid that they would lose their power—they said "no."

- Some were excited at the beginning, because they thought that he was about to set up the kingdom that they were hoping for - they were surprised.

- Some could see, by the grace of God. that Jesus was the one whom God had promised even though he seemed different than what their expectations were of him.

This is a key part of the journey—at some point every person needs to make a decision about who Jesus is and whether or not to follow him.

Leg Five–He Is Not Done

DAY TWENTY

What did Matthew tell us?

Now from the sixth hour there was darkness over all the land until the ninth hour. And about the ninth hour Jesus cried out with a loud voice, saying, "Eli, Eli, lema sabacthani?" that is, "My God, my God, why have you forsaken me?" And some of the bystanders, hearing it, said, "This man is calling Elijah." And one of them at once ran and took a sponge, filled it with sour wine, and put it on a reed and gave it to him to drink. But the others said, "Wait, let us see whether Elijah will come to save him." And Jesus cried out again with a loud voice and yielded up his spirit.

Matthew 27:45–50

When the Christmas season arrives, we prepare to celebrate the birth of Jesus. What a great story it is! A baby born to a young lady in a manger in Bethlehem. The angels shared the story with shepherds and celebrated. They also made sure that Herod didn't hurt him. Kings traveled far to see him. Everything seemed wonderful and amazing about this story.

And then, as the story continues, we come to a very different place. That baby grew up and focused on one message—the kingdom of God has come, and that a person needed to follow him to be a part of it. And for bringing that message, he was put to death on a terrible cross.

Some things to discuss

Does it seem like Jesus lost the battle, and that his enemies had won?

Was it hard for Jesus to die on the cross? What made him give up his life?

Ideas for parents: Have you kids taste some vinegar. Ask them to describe it and talk about whether they would want that sort of drink! Have them tell you what they think Jesus had to think about while he was on the cross.

DAY TWENTY-ONE

What did Matthew tell us?

Now after the Sabbath, toward the dawn of the first day of the week, Mary Magdalene and the other Mary went to see the tomb. And behold, there was a great earthquake, for an angel of the Lord descended from heaven and came and rolled back the stone and sat on it. His appearance was like lightning, and his clothing white as snow. And for fear of him the guards trembled and became like dead men. But the angel said to the women, "Do not be afraid, for I know that you seek Jesus who was crucified. He is not here, for he has risen, as he said. Come, see the place where he lay. Then go quickly and tell his disciples that he has risen from the dead, and behold, he is going before you to Galilee; there you will see him. See, I have told you." So they departed quickly from the tomb with fear and great joy, and ran to tell his disciples. And behold, Jesus met them and said, "Greetings!" And they came up and took hold of his feet and worshiped him. Then Jesus said to them, "Do not be afraid; go and tell my brothers to go to Galilee, and there they will see me."

Matthew 28:1–11

Once again, we need an angel to help us understand what is going on! And nothing could have been harder to understand than the idea that a man who had died a miserable death only three days earlier was now alive and talking with them. You can understand both their joy and their fear!

Some things to discuss

How do you think Jesus could rise from the dead?

What can we do now since he is alive?

DAY TWENTY-TWO

What did Matthew tell us?

Now the eleven disciples went to Galilee, to the mountain to which Jesus had directed them. And when they saw him they worshiped him, but some doubted. And Jesus came and said to them, "All authority in heaven and on earth has been given to me. Go therefore and make disciples of all nations, baptizing them in the name of the Father and of the Son and of the Holy Spirit, teaching them to observe all that I have commanded you. And behold, I am with you always, to the end of the age."

Matthew 28:16–20

In football, a common play is for the quarterback to hand the ball off to a running back, and then the entire opposing team would stop pursuing the quarterback and try and tackle the person with the ball. Since the day Jesus was baptized and the dove landed on his shoulder, Jesus had been leading the team as he began to explain to everyone that he was the Messiah and that being part of his kingdom wasn't about having a strong new government, but about being part of the eternal realm of God as he works out his grand plan of salvation.

In this passage, "the ball" is passed to the disciples—only it's not just a ball, it's a rescue story. God wants more people to be part of his kingdom. He wants more people to be forgiven and restored to how he created them. But Jesus' time to depart had come and he called on the rest of the team, the disciples who loved Jesus, to start the job of telling others what he had shared with them.

But there is something very different about this handoff. In football, the quarterback is out of the play. He just stops running and stays behind. Following Jesus is very different because he stays deep in our hearts and souls, and he works in us to keep the journey of his coming kingdom very active and alive.

Some things to discuss

We can't see Jesus. So how do we know if he is with us or not?

What could be more important than being part of God's kingdom?

DAY TWENTY-THREE

As we have celebrated this advent together, we have been trying to put ourselves in the same sandals that Matthew wore. He was a tax collector and hated by many of his fellow Jewish community members. But he was confronted by a man, Jesus, who reached out to him and asked him to follow. Learning from Jesus' teaching and being on the journey that Matthew had, not knowing where it would go, changed not only his life but also our history.

We can only imagine what inspired Matthew to write his gospel. But one thing we have seen together is that he wanted to show how intentional the God of the universe was in fulfilling the promise he made to Abraham back in Genesis about restoring creation back to the way he created it in the first place. God made that promise to Abraham and then, as the story unfolded, he used the prophets to help the people see, even when they were under terrific suffering, that a king would come who would surprisingly come as a baby born in a manger—Jesus.

As we close our study, it is important to know that there is more to come. The story of the king and the kingdom is not yet finished. A partner disciple with Matthew was a man named John, and he, like so many of the prophets we have read through so far, was also given a vision of something more to come. Here is what he shared:

> *Grace to you and peace from him who is and who was and who is to come, and from the seven spirits who are before his throne, and from Jesus Christ the faithful witness, the firstborn of the dead, and the ruler of kings on earth.*

To him who loves us and has freed us from our sins by
his blood and made us a kingdom, priests to his God and
Father, to him be glory and dominion forever and ever.
Amen. Behold, he is coming with the clouds, and every eye
will see him, even those who pierced him, and all tribes of
the earth will wail on account of him. Even so. Amen. "I am
the Alpha and the Omega," says the Lord God, "who is and
who was and who is to come, the Almighty."

Revelation 1:4–8

This is a prophecy that is yet to be fulfilled. Jesus will come again, and when the Almighty comes, he will restore what God created in the first place. The words "alpha" and "omega" come from the Greek alphabet. It is like saying "from A to Z." When God created the world, Jesus was there, and he will be there when the world will be restored. What Jesus asks us is the same question he posed to Matthew: Will you follow me? Can you trust me?

Some things to discuss

What is it like for you to look forward to Jesus coming again?

Ideas for parents: Have you kids write out the alphabet and then write a word for each letter that describes God.

LEG FIVE—HE IS NOT DONE

What did Matthew want us to understand about this part of Jesus' life? Leg Five sets the stage for all humans for all time—from Adam to the people who saw Jesus on earth, to us now. Those who thought that Jesus was not the promised king wanted to kill him so that they would be done with this problem and safeguard their positions as leaders from this threat.

But just like we saw in Leg One—God's hand holds Jesus. Just like God enabled Jesus to be born to a virgin, so also could God raise him from the grave. Absolutely nothing can stop the plan that God has for establishing his kingdom in and through Jesus.

And now there remains one more Leg. It's your Leg of the journey. It's not likely that you will know what that will be like—Jesus is always full of surprises. It might be different than what other people think—many people disagreed with Jesus. It might seem like the days are dark—like they were when Jesus was dead on a cross.

But no matter what your Leg could be like, one thing is true. Jesus loves you so much that one day you will see him face to face.

What do you want your journey to be about?

Remember Where We Started!

DAY TWENTY-FOUR

This is our last advent day. We have learned much together. Thank you for joining in the journey! Let's just take a moment to see the wonderful hand of God as he changed the course of the world by giving us His Son.

> *In those days a decree went out from Caesar Augustus that all the world should be registered. This was the first registration when Quirinius was governor of Syria. And all went to be registered, each to his own town. And Joseph also went up from Galilee, from the town of Nazareth, to Judea, to the city of David, which is called Bethlehem, because he was of the house and lineage of David, to be registered with Mary, his betrothed, who was with child. And while they were there, the time came for her to give birth. And she gave birth to her firstborn son and wrapped him in swaddling cloths and laid him in a manger, because there was no place for them in the inn.*

And in the same region there were shepherds out in the field, keeping watch over their flock by night. And an angel of the Lord appeared to them, and the glory of the Lord shone around them, and they were filled with great fear. And the angel said to them, "Fear not, for behold, I bring you good news of great joy that will be for all the people. For unto you is born this day in the city of David a Savior, who is Christ the Lord. And this will be a sign for you: you will find a baby wrapped in swaddling cloths and lying in a manger." And suddenly there was with the angel a multitude of the heavenly host praising God and saying, "Glory to God in the highest, and on earth peace among those with whom he is pleased!"

When the angels went away from them into heaven, the shepherds said to one another, "Let us go over to Bethlehem and see this thing that has happened, which the Lord has made known to us." And they went with haste and found Mary and Joseph, and the baby lying in a manger. And when they saw it, they made known the saying that had been told them concerning this child. And all who heard it wondered at what the shepherds told them. But Mary treasured up all these things, pondering them in her heart. And the shepherds returned, glorifying and praising God for all they had heard and seen, as it had been told them.

Luke 2:1–20

MERRY CHRISTMAS!